BUILDING BLOCKS OF MATH

GEOMETRIC MEASUREMENT

Written by Regina Osweiller

Illustrated by Daniel Hawkins

WORLD BOOK

a Scott Fetzer company
Chicago

World Book, Inc.
180 North LaSalle Street
Suite 900
Chicago, Illinois 60601
USA

For information about other World Book publications, visit our website at **www.worldbook.com** or call **1-800-WORLDBK (967-5325).**
For information about sales to schools and libraries, call 1-800-975-3250 (United States), or 1-800-837-5365 (Canada).

WORLD BOOK STAFF
Executive Committee
President: Geoff Broderick
Vice President, Editorial: Tom Evans
Vice President, Finance: Donald D. Keller
Vice President, Marketing: Jean Lin
Vice President, International: Eddy Kisman
Vice President, Technology: Jason Dole
Director, Human Resources: Bev Ecker

Editorial
Manager, New Content: Jeff De La Rosa
Associate Manager, New Product: Nicholas Kilzer
Sr. Editor: William M. Harrod
Proofreader: Nathalie Strassheim

Graphics and Design
Sr. Visual Communications Designer: Melanie Bender
Sr. Web Designer/Digital Media Developer: Matt Carrington

Library of Congress Cataloging-in-Publication Data for this volume has been applied for.

Building Blocks of Math
ISBN: 978-0-7166-4253-4 (set, hc.)

Geometric Measurement
ISBN: 978-0-7166-4258-9 (hc.)

Also available as:
ISBN: 978-0-7166-4268-8 (e-book)

Printed in India by Thomson Press (India) Limited, Uttar Pradesh, India
1st printing June 2022

Acknowledgments:
Writer: Regina Osweiller
Illustrator: Daniel Hawkins/The Bright Agency
Colorist: Leo Trinidad/The Bright Agency
Series Advisor: Marjorie Frank
Special thanks to KnowledgeWorks Global Ltd.

TABLE OF CONTENTS

THE ADVENTURE BEGINS!
For Three and Eight, adventures in reading begin at the Number City Library. But who is the new librarian, and what adventures will he launch?
Let's see, a math book called *Measurement in Geometry* ...
an adventure book, *Iowa James and the Golden Circle* ..
and from our cooking and baking collection, *1001 Fun Birthday Cakes.* All these are due in three weeks.
MEASUREMENT IN GEOMETRY
IOWA JAMES AND THE GOLDEN CIRCLE
1001 FUN BIRTHDAY CAKES
1001 FUN BIRTHDAY CAKES
BOOK BAG
Thank you.
But be warned! Don't trip over the book bag while drinking strawberry-apple fruit juice and trying to catch a basketball!
BAM
Have a nice day.
FRONT DESK
BOOK RETURN

FRUIT JUICE
TODAY'S SPECIAL
STRAWBERRY APPLE
Three, do you think this is a good idea?
Don't be silly, Eight. That odd librarian was just trying to scare us into-
Hey, look out!
17
BOOK BAG
TRIP!
1001 FUN BIRTHDAY CAKES
WHOOSH!
MEASUREMENT IN GEOMETRY
IOWA JAMES AND THE GOLDEN CIRCLE

POLYGONS AND PERIMETER
POLYGON LAND
So, you wanted an adventure? Well, you've got one!
What happened? Why are we wearing these clothes?
You have entered the combined world of the three books you borrowed.
Before you can return to your regular lives, you must find the perfect, flawless Lost Golden Circle and calculate its circumference and area.
Good luck! If you need me, I'll be at the front desk.
How do we get to the front–

Could a circle be in Polygon Land?
No way! Circles are round.
A **polygon** is a two-dimensional figure enclosed by straight sides and angles. I am a pentagon, meaning I have five sides and five angles. Here are other polygons.
Nice to meet all of you.
QUADRILATERALS: Polygons with four sides
Trapezoid a quadrilateral with only one pair of parallel sides
Pentagon a polygon with five sides
Parallelogram a quadrilateral with two pairs of parallel sides of equal length opposite equal angles
Parallel lines never meet. My parallel sides are opposite each other.
Rectangle a parallelogram with four right angles
Right angles are shown by corner marks.
Rhombus a parallelogram with four sides of equal length
Square a parallelogram with four sides of equal length and four right angles
Hexagon a polygon with six sides
Octagon a polygon with eight sides

What do we do now?
I guess we should start looking for the Golden Circle.
PERIMETER FESTIVAL
But it's the Perimeter Festival!
Uh ... what's a perimeter?
A **perimeter** is the distance around a figure. Before you are allowed to leave the festival, you must find the perimeters of several polygons.
I am a **regular polygon**, meaning I have equal side lengths and equal angles. My perimeter is 4 x 4, or 16 centimeters.
4cm
Someone did not pay attention to the stop sign–another regular polygon!
75cm
3cm
3cm
3cm
8cm
8cm
4cm
STOP

I'm a regular polygon!
3cm
I'm an **irregular polygon**, meaning that not all my side lengths and angles sizes are equal. 6 + 4 + 3 + 5 = 18, so my perimeter is 18 centimeters.
3cm
4cm
5cm
6cm
6cm
5cm
8cm
Can you readers help Three and Eight find the perimeters of the polygons on pages 8 and 9 that show measurements?
Perimeter of a regular polygon = *ns*
n = number of sides
s = side length
For the regular polygons, including me, use the formula above. For the irregular polygons, add the side lengths to find the perimeter.
5cm
See page 40 for the answers.

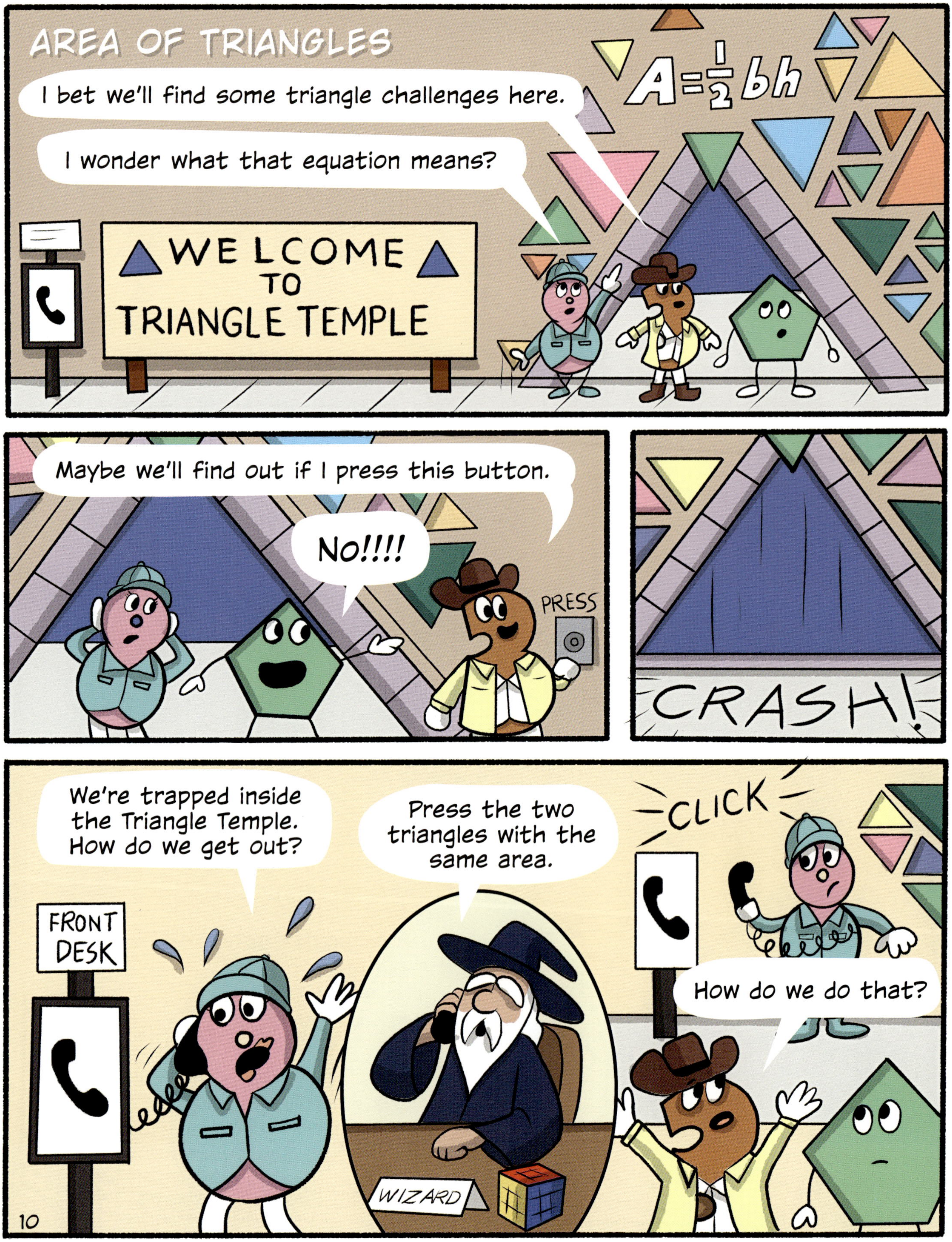
AREA OF TRIANGLES
$A = \frac{1}{2}bh$
I bet we'll find some triangle challenges here.
I wonder what that equation means?
WELCOME TO TRIANGLE TEMPLE
Maybe we'll find out if I press this button.
No!!!!
PRESS
CRASH!
We're trapped inside the Triangle Temple. How do we get out?
FRONT DESK
Press the two triangles with the same area.
WIZARD
CLICK
How do we do that?

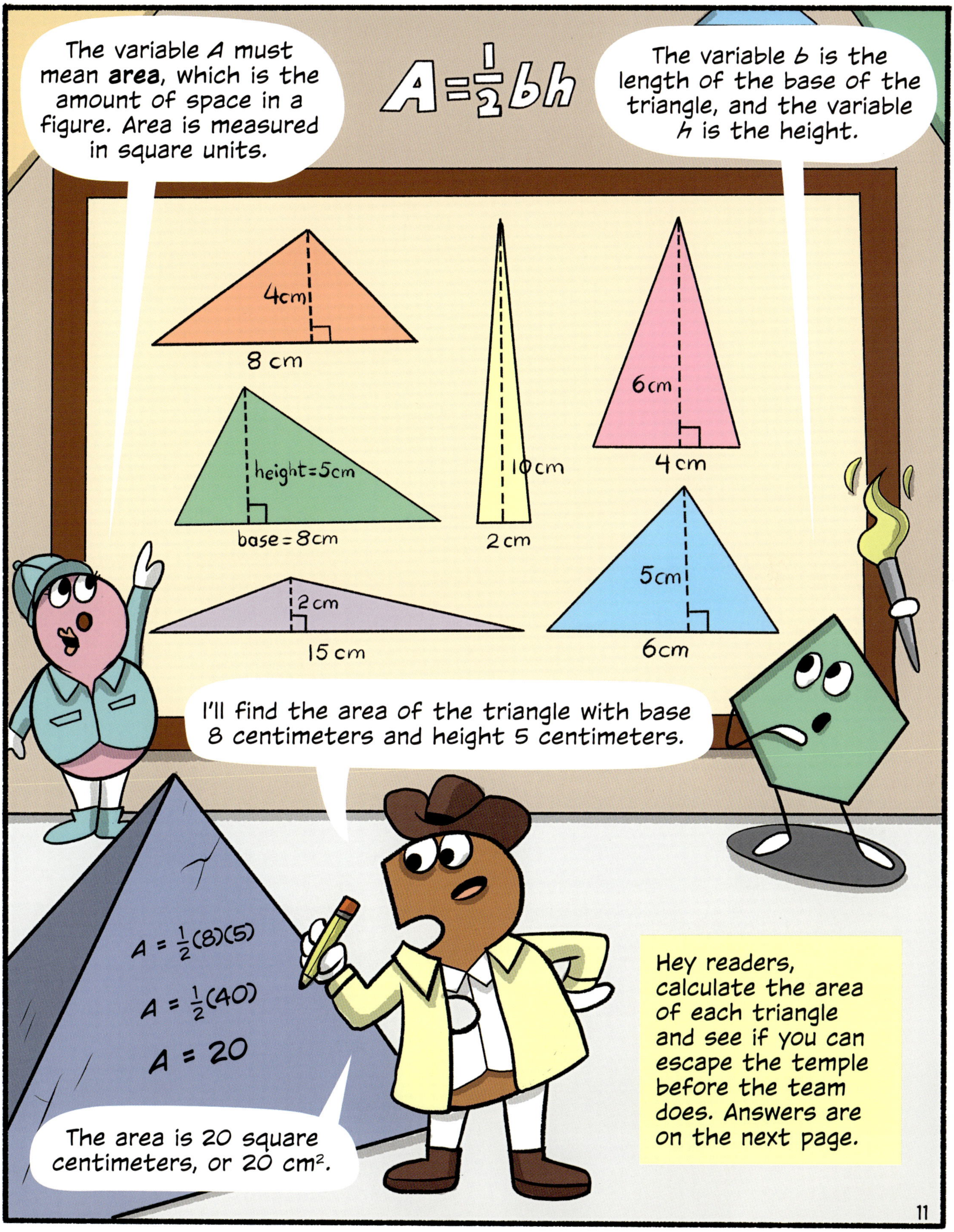
The variable A must mean **area**, which is the amount of space in a figure. Area is measured in square units.
$A = \frac{1}{2}bh$
The variable b is the length of the base of the triangle, and the variable h is the height.
4cm
8 cm
10cm
2 cm
6cm
4 cm
height=5cm
base=8cm
5cm
6cm
2 cm
15 cm
I'll find the area of the triangle with base 8 centimeters and height 5 centimeters.
$A = \frac{1}{2}(8)(5)$
$A = \frac{1}{2}(40)$
$A = 20$
The area is 20 square centimeters, or 20 cm^2.
Hey readers, calculate the area of each triangle and see if you can escape the temple before the team does. Answers are on the next page.

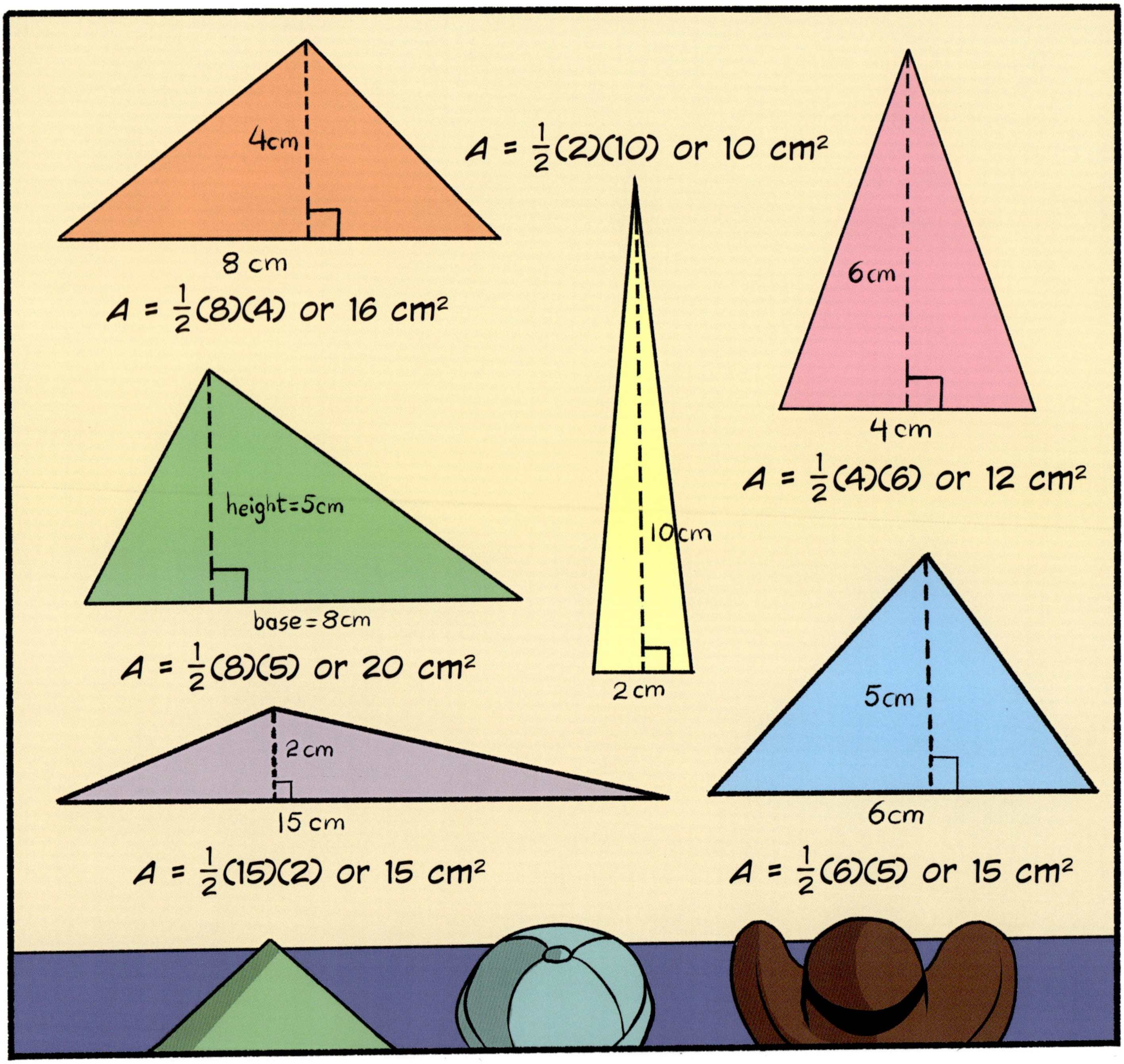
4cm
8 cm
A = 1/2(8)(4) or 16 cm²
A = 1/2(2)(10) or 10 cm²
10cm
2 cm
6cm
4 cm
A = 1/2(4)(6) or 12 cm²
height=5cm
base=8cm
A = 1/2(8)(5) or 20 cm²
2 cm
15 cm
A = 1/2(15)(2) or 15 cm²
5cm
6cm
A = 1/2(6)(5) or 15 cm²

Great! You found two triangles with the same 15-square-centimeter area!

See page 40 for the answers.

AREA OF SQUARES AND RECTANGLES

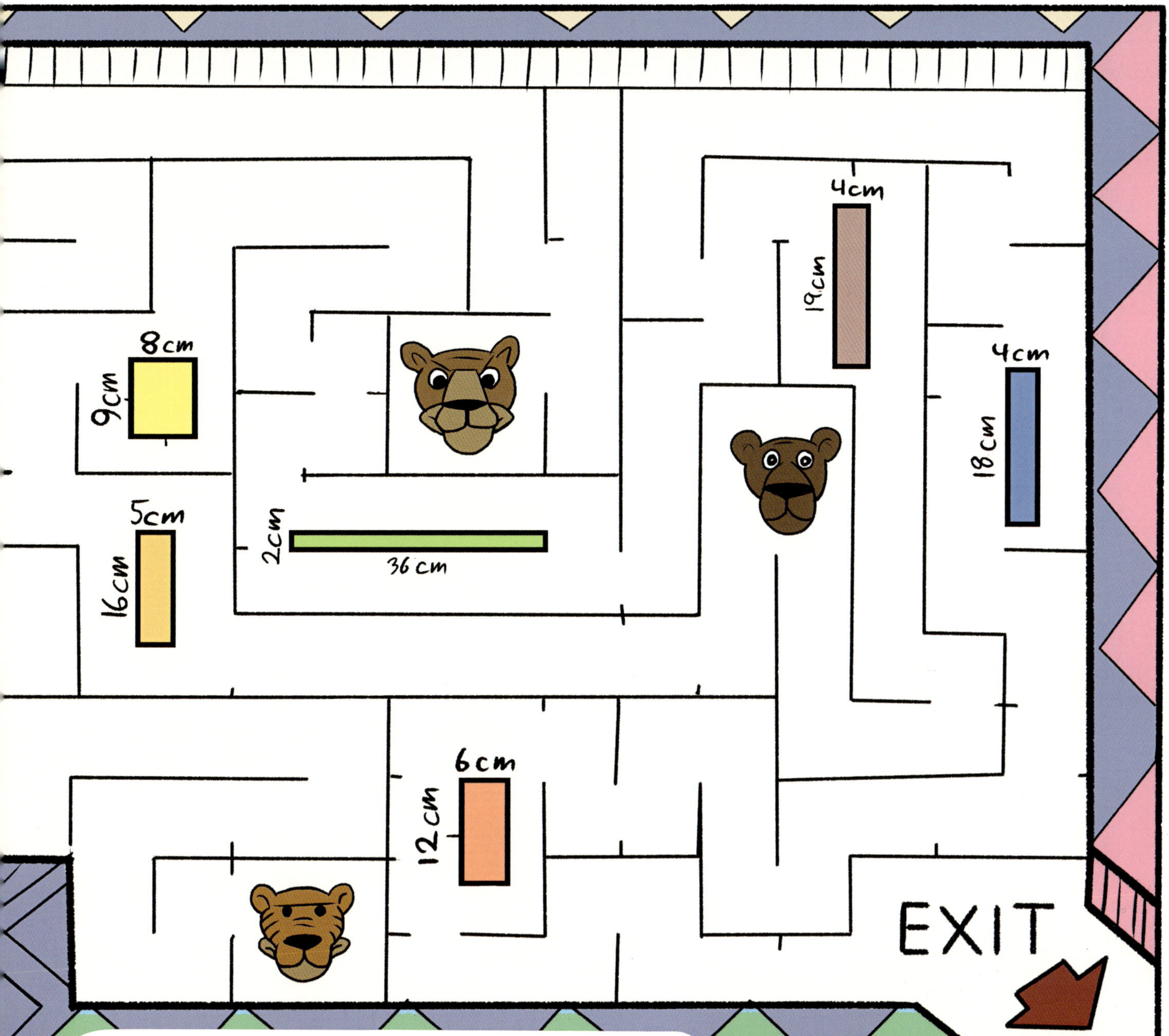

Find the missing side length for these squares and rectangles. The first problem is solved for you.

1. Rectangle of area 16 cm², length 8 cm
   16 = 8w
   w = 2
   The width is 2 cm.
2. Rectangle of area 36 m², width 9 m
3. Square of area 36 cm²
4. Rectangle of area 24 cm², width 3 cm

See page 40 for the answers.

AREA OF COMPOSITE FIGURES
Congratulations on finding the areas of triangles, squares, and rectangles. Now before continuing your quest, you'll need to find the areas of the composite figures in Tiger Village.
Composite figures are combinations of simpler figures.
When I draw this dotted line, the figure is divided into two rectangles that do not overlap.
The total area is the sum of the two areas, or 140 square centimeters.
10cm
10cm
9cm
5cm
20cm
Area of left rectangle:
9 x 10 = 90 or 90 cm²
Area of right rectangle:
5 x 10 = 50 or 50 cm²
Total area:
140 cm²
MARSHMALLOWS

See page 40 for the answers.

Hmm, this composite figure looks like a rectangle with a triangle cut out of it.
We can find the area of both the whole rectangle and triangle, and then subtract to find the area of the figure!
9m
8m
3m
4m
The area is 66 square meters. Here's how we found that:
Area of outer rectangle:
A = lw
= (8)(9)
= 72 m²
Area of triangle:
A = ½bh
= ½(4)(3)
= 6 m²
Area of figure: 72 - 6 or 66 m²
Whew! We passed that challenge. Now, when are we going to find some circles?

See page 40 for the answers.

AREA OF PARALLELOGRAMS WITH NO RIGHT ANGLES
Welcome to the Cave of Parallelograms! To pass through the cave, you must find the parallelogram with an area of 21 square centimeters.
How do we calculate the area of parallelograms?
According to the ancient guidebook of my people, the area of a parallelogram is the product of the base and the height.
MEASUREMENT IN GEOMETRY
Hey! That's the geometry book I checked out of the library!
The height is the distance between two parallel bases.
Parallelograms
A = bh
A: area
b: base
h: height
b
h
Remember to return that book in three weeks!

Readers, use the formula to find the area of each parallelogram.
3 cm
8cm
9 cm
4 cm
height = 6 cm
base = 12 cm
7 cm
3 cm
A = bh
= (6)(12)
= 72
The area is 72 cm².
See page 40 for the answers.

AREA OF TRAPEZOIDS
7cm
3cm
A = (3)(7)
= 21
Area is 21 cm²
You found the area of parallelograms. And for your next challenge ... find the area of trapezoids.
Aren't you the same tiger who guarded the other cave?
Here's the formula for the area of a trapezoid.
b1
h
b2
Trapezoids
A = ½(b1 + b2)h
A: area
b1: short base length
b2: long base length
h: height
The two bases are the parallel sides. The height is the distance between them.

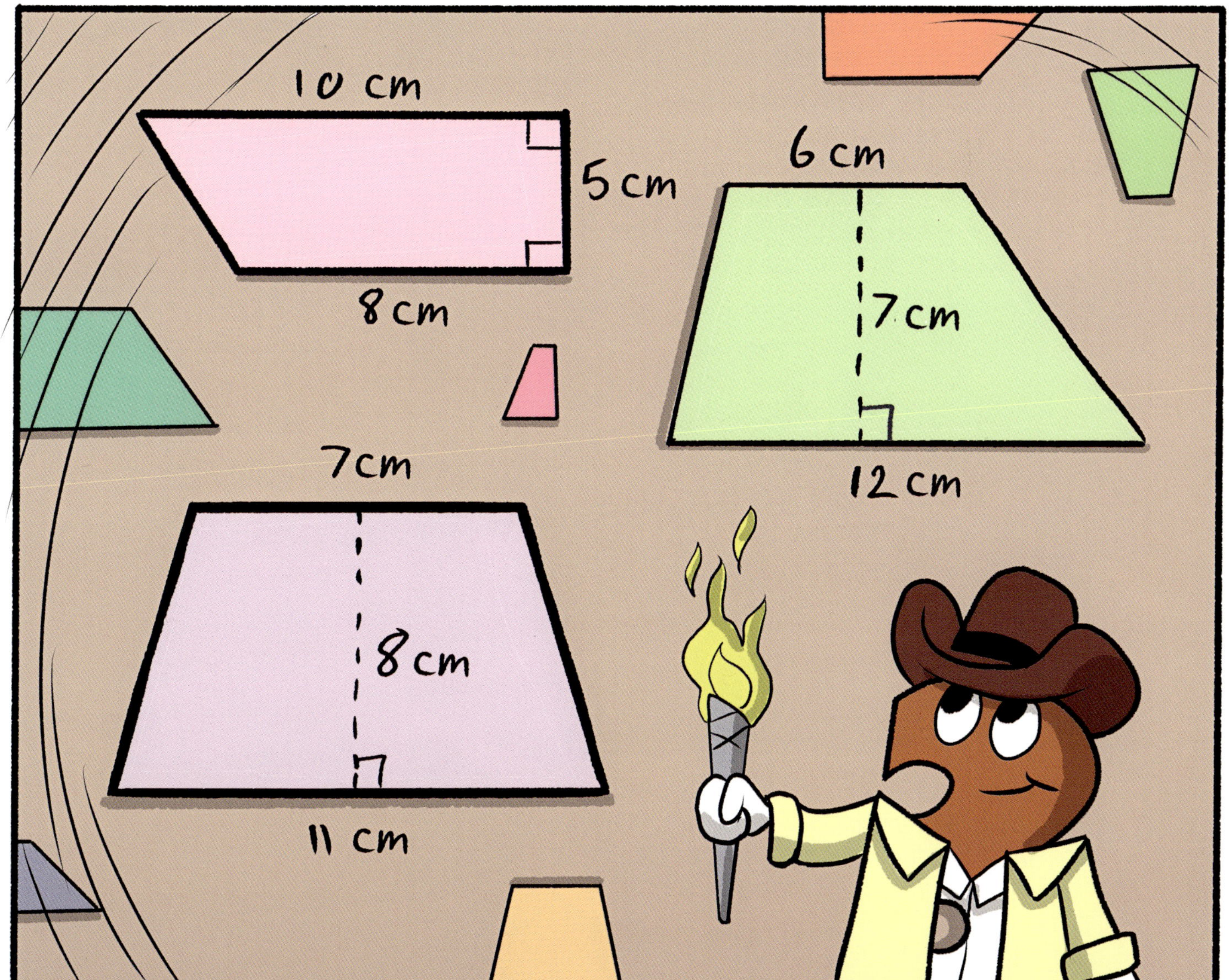

See page 40 for the answers.

Wow! Now where are we?
At least I don't see any tigers!
This is the coordinate plane where figures are plotted on a grid. Each of the grid lines is numbered, beginning with 0. We must find the area of each rectangle for the snakes to let us pass!
We can find each area by counting the little squares inside them. There are 12 squares in the red rectangle, so its area is 12 square units.
0
1
2
3
4
5
6
7
8
9
10
11
12
1
2
3

Reader, find the area of each shape outlined in color. Also, find the perimeter of each rectangle. Do this by starting at one corner and counting the grid lines around the figure until you get back to the beginning corner.

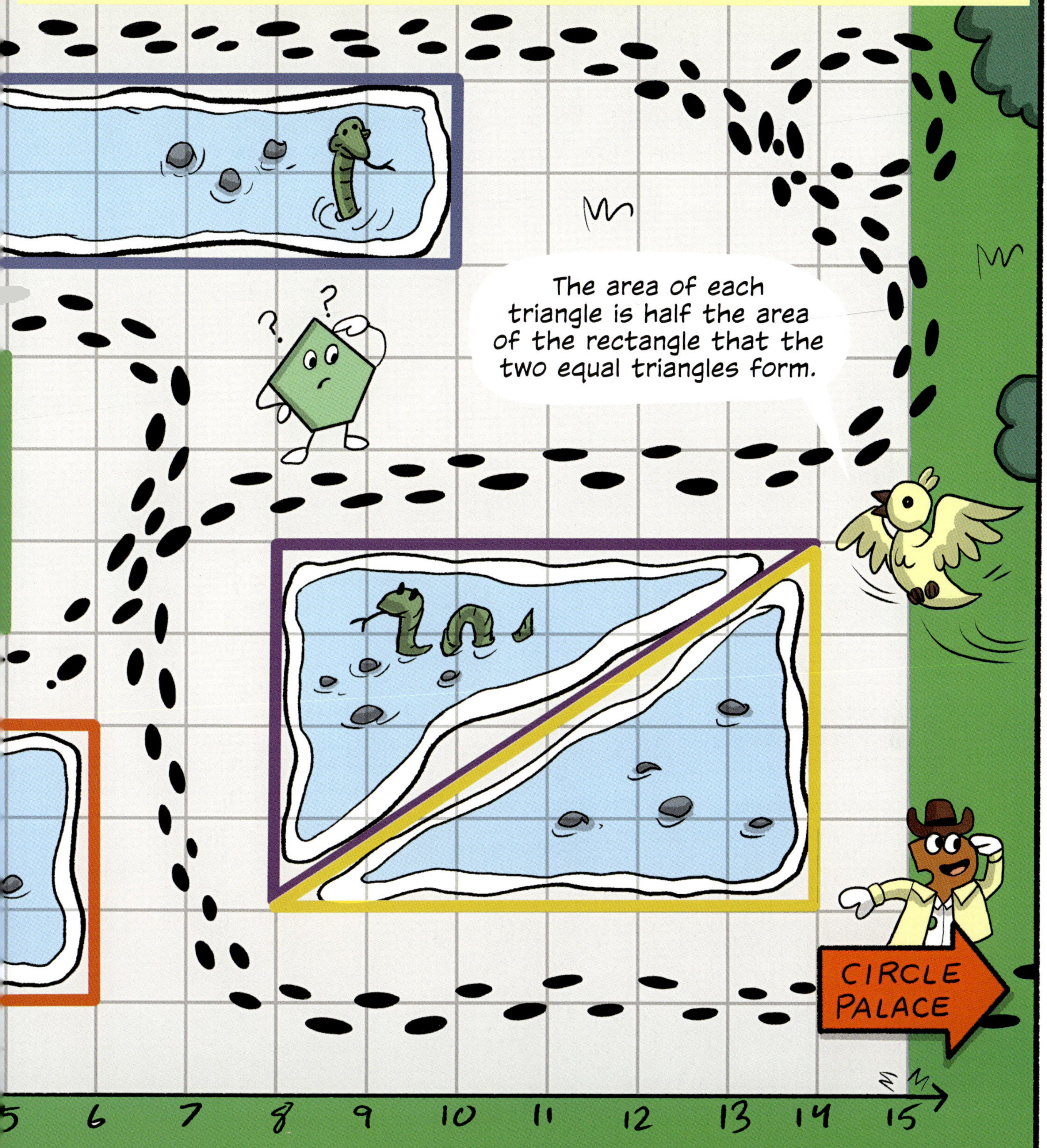

See page 40 for the answers.

CIRCLE MEASUREMENTS
CIRCLE PALACE
It seems that we have left Polygon Land. I see a lot of curved lines!
Maybe we're getting closer to the Golden Circle.
Look at all the circles here in the Circle Palace! They're two-dimensional figures like me, but they're not polygons. Remember, they have no sides or angles!
COOKIE SALE
The **diameter** is the distance across a circle through its center.
The **radius** is the distance from the center of a circle to any point on its edge. The radius is one half the diameter.
The **circumference** of a circle is the distance around it. You can measure the circumference with a piece of string and a ruler.
Diameter d: 5 cm
Circumference C: about 15.7 cm
Ratio $\frac{C}{d} \approx 3.14$ cm
$\approx$
This symbol means "approximately equal to."

Wow, that's the Greek letter *pi*! They say its digits go on forever and never repeat.
$\pi = 3.14159265...$
That's right. Pi is very important to us circles. For a circle of any size, pi is the ratio of the circumference to the diameter. For convenience in solving problems, we generally round pi to the hundredth place: 3.14.

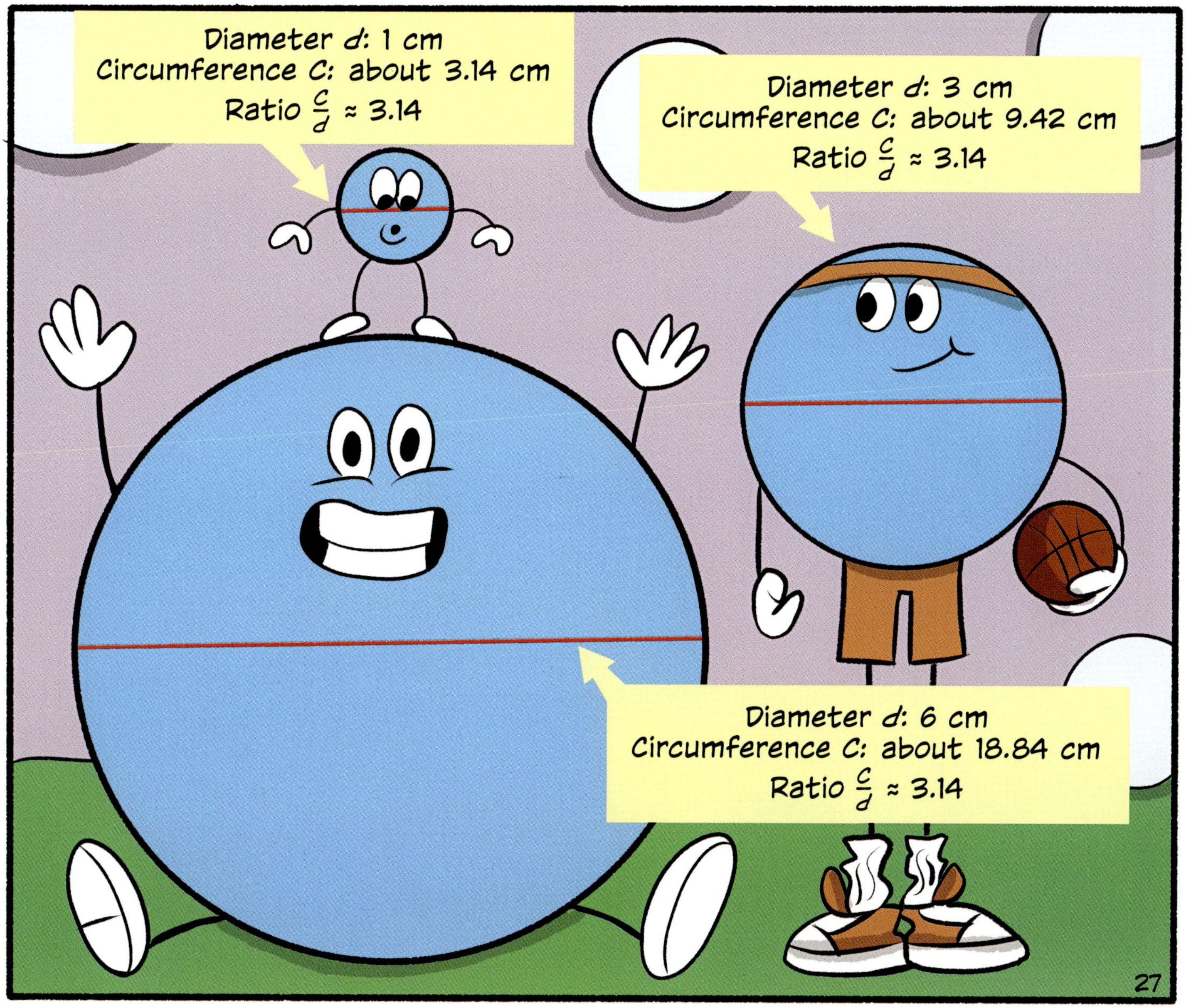
Diameter d: 1 cm
Circumference C: about 3.14 cm
Ratio $\frac{C}{d} \approx 3.14$
Diameter d: 3 cm
Circumference C: about 9.42 cm
Ratio $\frac{C}{d} \approx 3.14$
Diameter d: 6 cm
Circumference C: about 18.84 cm
Ratio $\frac{C}{d} \approx 3.14$

All visitors to the Circle Palace must calculate the circumference and area of several circles.
We're game for that!
Use pi to calculate the circumference and area of a circle. Use 3.14 for pi. Notice that since the diameter is twice the radius, the circumference is also the product of 2r (twice the radius) and pi.
Circumference of a circle: $c = \pi d$, or $2\pi r$
Area of a circle: $A = \pi r^2$

Your diameter is 4 centimeters, so your circumference is 4π, or about 12.6 centimeters.
c = πd ≈ (3.14)(4) ≈ 12.56
A = πr² ≈ (3.14)(3²) ≈ (3.14)9 ≈ 28.26
Your radius is 3 centimeters, so your area is 9π, or about 28.3 square centimeters.
4cm
3 cm
7cm
Look! It's the Lost Golden Circle! We found it!
Readers, can you find the circumference and area of the circle that Three discovered? Turn the page to check your answer.

VOLUME OF RECTANGULAR PRISMS
Circumference = 14π, or about 44 cm
Area = 49π, or about 154 cm²
7cm
I'm afraid you're too late!
You're the number who threw the basketball at us!
That's right! After I found the circumference and area of the Golden Circle, the people here were so impressed that they crowned me as their queen.
1001 FUN BIRTHDAY CAKES
Now, my first command is ... bake me a birthday cake!
A birthday cake?
?
The third book in the book bag.
I decree that the volume of the cake be 24 cubic meters, which should be enough to feed everybody.

A few moments later ...
Polyhedron Kitchen
I am Chef Tetrahedron. This is my kitchen. Here we bake cakes in the shape of **polyhedra**, which are three-dimensional shapes formed from polygon faces.
Our cake is in the shape of a **rectangular prism**, which is a polyhedron with 6 rectangular faces.
ICING
The volume of a rectangular prism is the product of its length, width, and height.
The volume of three-dimensional figures is always measured in cubic units.
4m
3m
2m
So the volume of the cake is 3 x 2 x 4, or 24 cubic meters.
Volume of a rectangular prism = length x width x height.

Readers, can you find the volume of each rectangular prism shown here? The first volume is calculated for you.
V = lwh
= (6)(8)(4)
= 192 cm^3
6 cm
8 cm
4cm
5cm
5cm
5cm
A
17
4cm
9 cm
6cm
3cm
6cm
7cm
See page 40 for the answers.

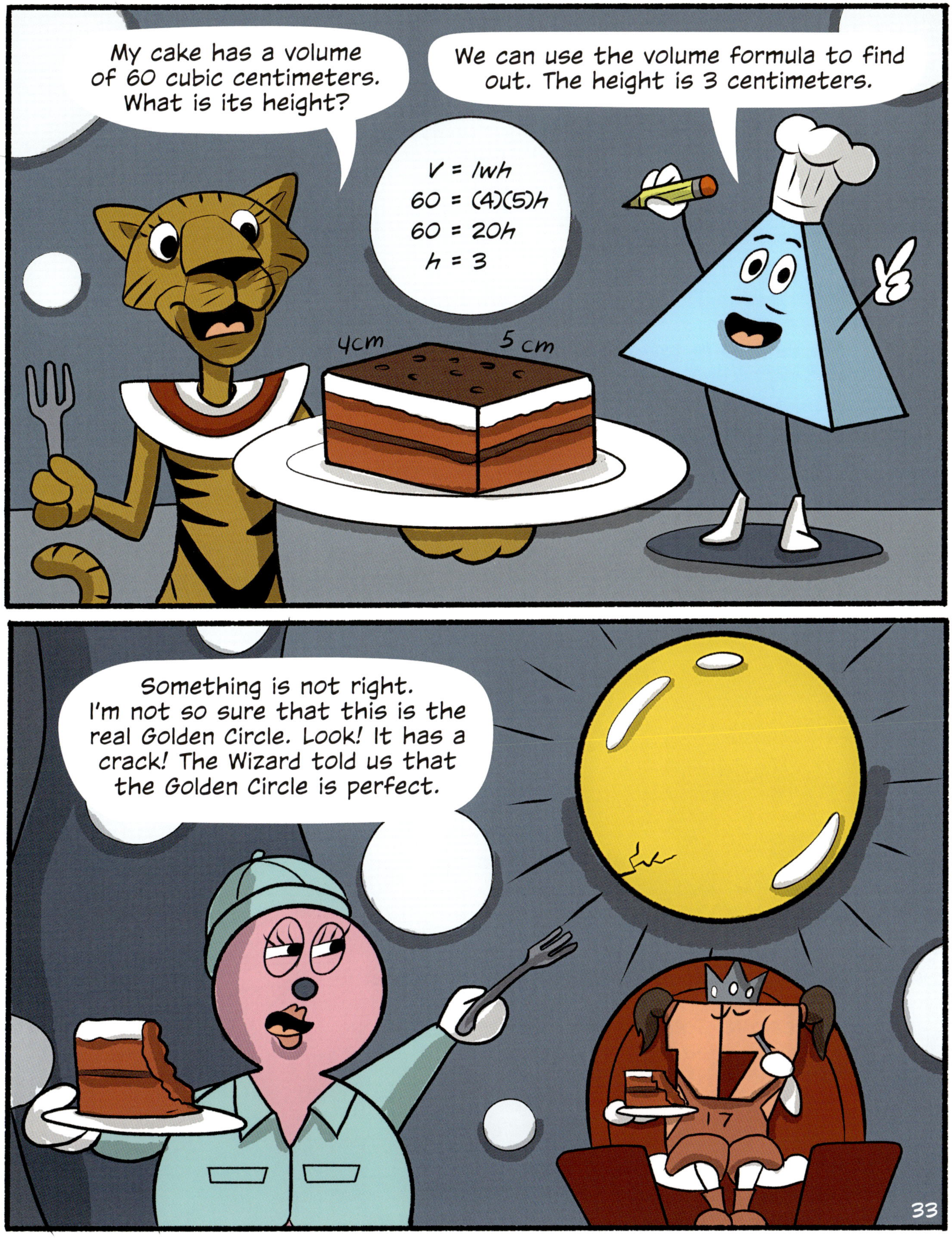
My cake has a volume of 60 cubic centimeters. What is its height?
We can use the volume formula to find out. The height is 3 centimeters.
V = lwh
60 = (4)(5)h
60 = 20h
h = 3
4cm
5 cm
Something is not right. I'm not so sure that this is the real Golden Circle. Look! It has a crack! The Wizard told us that the Golden Circle is perfect.

MEASUREMENT PROBLEMS
Hey! Here's another golden circle.
Maybe this is the real one that we're supposed to find.
I don't see any flaws in it!
The area of the large rectangle is the product of its length and width, which is 240 square centimeters.
But the area of the blue section is 204 square centimeters, so the difference must be the area of the red square: 36 square centimeters.
10cm
24 cm
Blue Rectangle, Red Square, Golden Circle!
Area shaded blue: 204 cm²
Circumference of circle:
?
Area of circle:
?

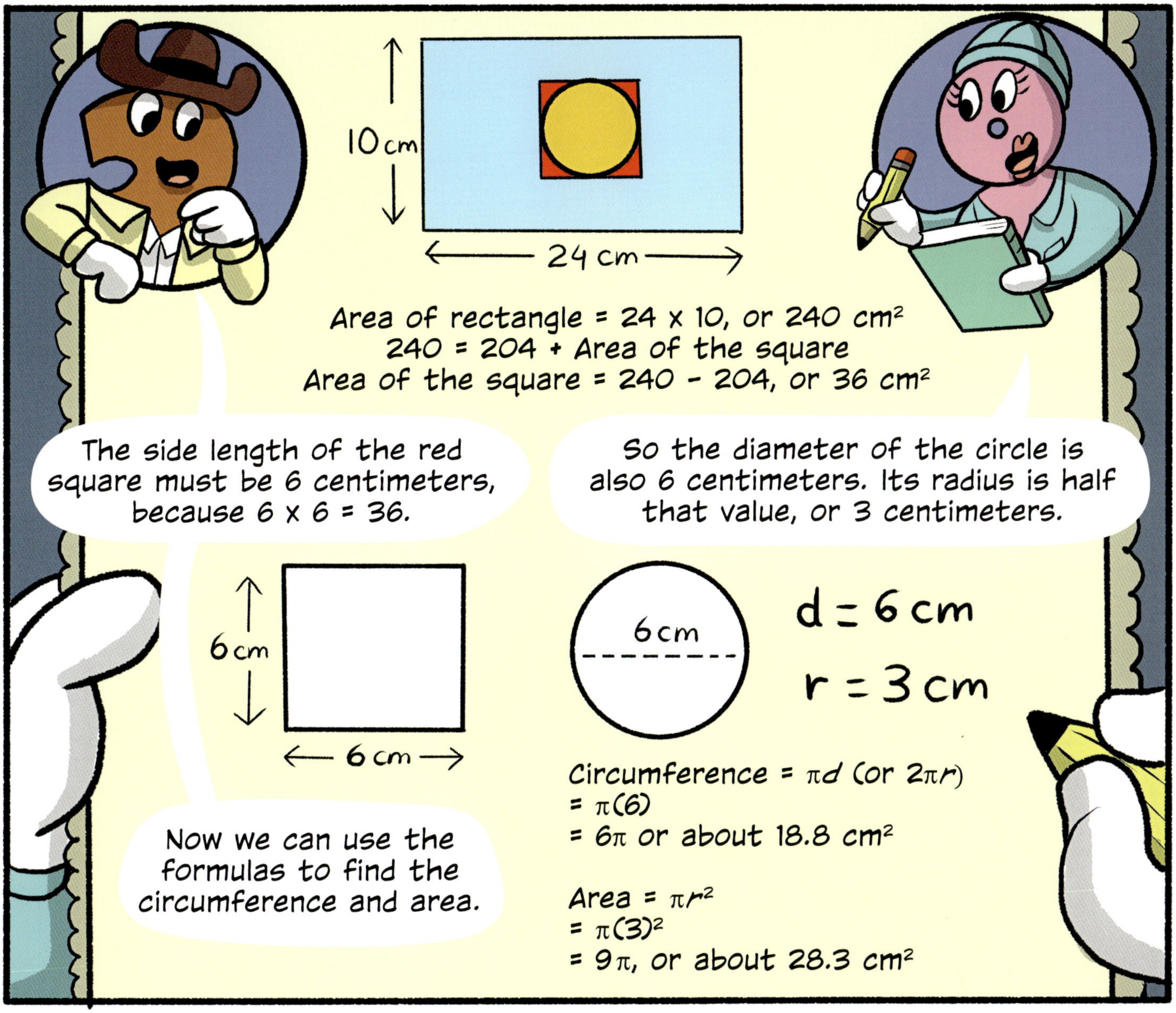
10 cm
24 cm
Area of rectangle = 24 x 10, or 240 cm^2
240 = 204 + Area of the square
Area of the square = 240 - 204, or 36 cm^2
The side length of the red square must be 6 centimeters, because 6 x 6 = 36.
So the diameter of the circle is also 6 centimeters. Its radius is half that value, or 3 centimeters.
6 cm
6 cm
6 cm
d = 6 cm
r = 3 cm
Now we can use the formulas to find the circumference and area.
Circumference = πd (or $2\pi r$)
= $\pi(6)$
= 6π or about 18.8 cm^2
Area = πr^2
= $\pi(3)^2$
= 9π, or about 28.3 cm^2

I hope this works!
Circumference of circle:
about 18.8 cm
Area of circle:
about 28.3 cm^2?
WHOOOOSH!

MORE MEASUREMENT PROBLEMS
We did it! We made it home!
Hey! Check this out.
1001 FUN BIRTHDAY CAKES
Golden Circle Birthday Cake
with blue, red, and golden frosting

Hey readers! Can you solve these problems?
GO TEAM!
6cm
5cm
WE'RE #1
First, compare the perimeters of these two flags. Each flag is a regular polygon.
Second problem: a semicircle is half of a circle. What is the area of this semicircle?
17
2m
5cm
3cm
3cm
FRUIT JUICE
3cm
4cm
4cm
Finally, which fruit juice box has the greater volume? Both are rectangular prisms.
See page 40 for the answers.
Remember, those books are due in three weeks. Don't be late!
Oh, do you charge a stiff fine?
BOOK BAG
You don't want to know!

SHOW WHAT YOU KNOW

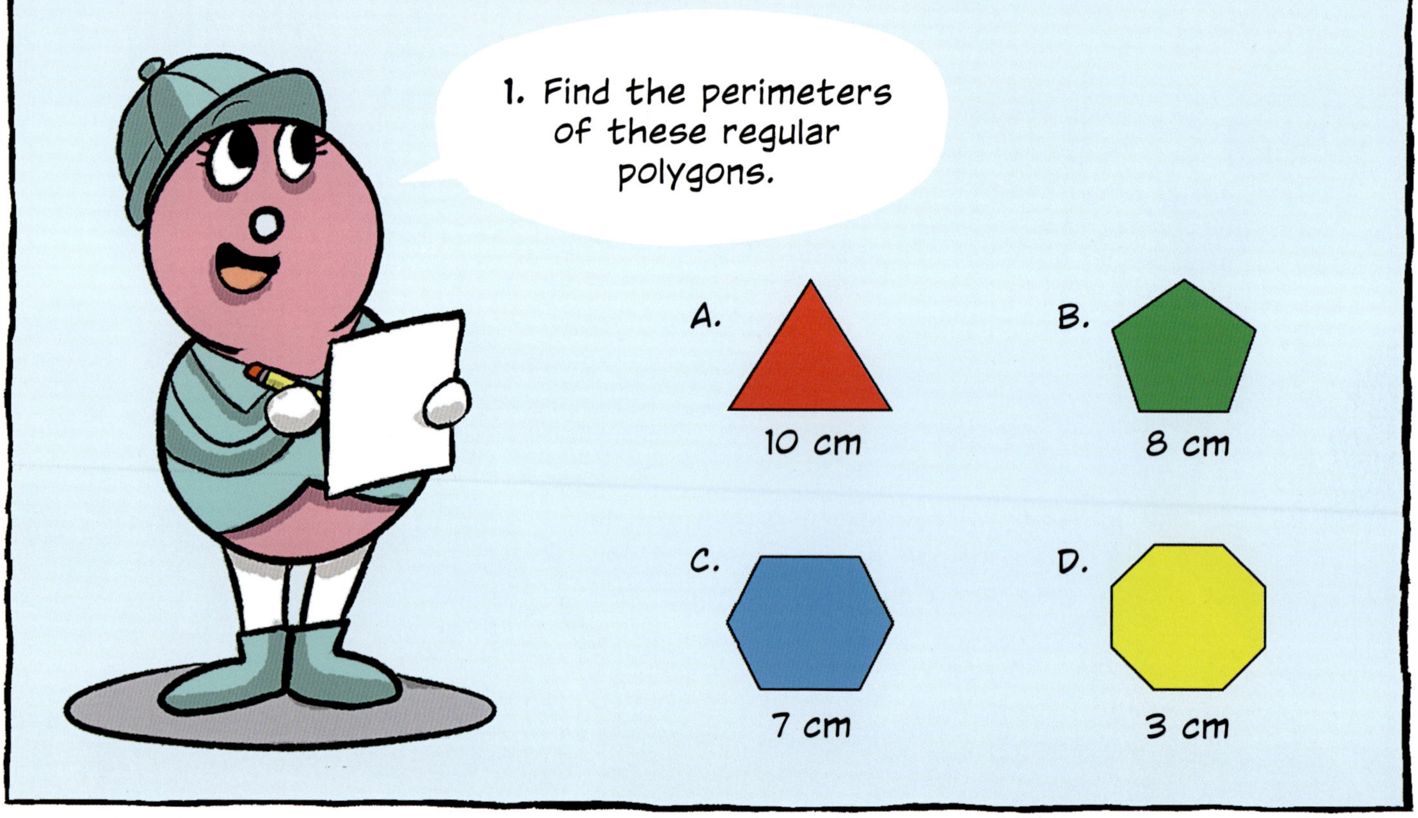

4. Multiple choice.
Choose the best answer for each question.

1. What is the area of a trapezoid with bases 6 m and 10 m and a height of 13 m?
   A. 78 m^2
   B. 104 m^2
   C. 130 m^2

2. What is the approximate area of a circle with a radius of 6 cm?
   A. 37.68 cm^2
   B. 113.04 cm^2
   C. 452.16 cm^2

3. What is the base of a triangle whose area is 20 m^2 and whose height is 10 cm?
   A. 2 cm
   B. 3 cm
   C. 4 cm

4. Which of these figures does NOT have four sides of equal length?
   A. rectangle
   B. square
   C. trapezoid

See page 40 for answers.

ANSWERS

Page 8:
Purple triangle = 9 cm
Yellow triangle = 20 cm
Stop sign = 600 cm

Page 9:
Yellow hexagon = 18 cm
Blue triangle = 19 cm
Green pentagon = 20 cm

Page 13:
1. base = 2 cm
2. height = 4 cm
3. base = 4 cm
4. height = 18 m

Page 15:
1. width = 2 cm
2. base = 4 cm
3. side = 6 cm
4. base = 8 cm

Page 17:
Orange figure = 625 cm^2
Blue figure = 189 cm^2

Page 19:
Green figure = 76 cm^2
Yellow figure = 144 cm^2

Page 21:
Green parallelogram = 24 cm^2
Pink parallelogram = 36 cm^2
Yellow parallelogram = 72 cm^2
Blue parallelogram = 21 cm^2

Page 23:
Pink trapezoid = 45 cm^2
Green trapezoid = 63 cm^2
Purple trapezoid = 72 cm^2

Pages 24 and 25:
Blue rectangle:
area = 16 square units,
perimeter = 20 units
Green rectangle:
area = 12 square units,
perimeter = 14 units
Orange rectangle:
area = 12 square units,
perimeter = 14 units
Purple and yellow triangles:
each have area = 12 square units

Page 32:
Blue circle's cake = 125 cm^3
Eight's cake = 216 cm^3
Pentagon's cake = 126 cm^3

Page 37:
41's flags:
The flags both have the same perimeter, 30 cm.
17's semicircle:
1π, or about 3.1 m^2
9's fruit juices:
the banana-grape juice (48 cm^3) has a greater volume than the strawberry-apple juice (45 cm^3)

SHOW WHAT YOU KNOW
Pages 38-39:

1. A. The red triangle has a perimeter of 30 cm (3 sides x 10 cm = 30 cm).

B. The green pentagon has a perimeter of 40 cm (5 sides x 8 cm = 40 cm).

C. The blue hexagon has a perimeter of 42 cm (6 sides x 7 cm = 42 cm).

D. The yellow octagon has a perimeter of 24 cm (8 sides x 3 cm = 24 cm)

2. To find the volume of the birthday cake, multiply the length x width x height. The volume of the cake is (10)(8)(15) = 1,200 cm^3.

3. To find the area of the figure, first divide the figure into a 15 cm x 10 cm rectangle and a 15 cm x 10 cm triangle. The rectangle has an area of 150 cm^2 [(15)(10) = 150 cm^2]. The triangle has an area of 75 cm^2 [$\frac{1}{2}$ (15)(10) = 75 cm^2]. Adding the two figures gives a total of 225 cm^2.

4. 1. B, the area of a trapezoid is $\frac{1}{2}(6 + 10)(13) = 104$ m^2

2. B, the area of the circle is $3.14(6^2)$ which is about 113.04 cm^2

3. C, the area of a triangle is $\frac{1}{2}$ bh. Substituting the values, we have $20 = \frac{1}{2}(b)(10)$. Solving for b, we get b = 4 cm.

4. C, the trapezoid does NOT have four sides of equal length